In Heaven's Name, Why on Earth?

Crossways International
Minneapolis, MN

IN HEAVEN'S NAME, WHY ON EARTH?
was developed and written by
Harry Wendt, Minneapolis, MN

Illustrations by Knarelle Beard, Adelaide, South Australia

IN HEAVEN'S NAME, WHY ON EARTH?
is published and distributed by
CROSSWAYS INTERNATIONAL
7930 Computer Avenue South
Minneapolis, MN 55435-5415

Contents

Foreword

When producing materials on stewardship for use in Christendom, it is customary to rehash traditional explanations of 1 Corinthians 16:2, relate the matter entirely to giving money to "church structures," and suggest:

- Each person should *give*.

- God's *share* should be set aside *first*.

- Each person should give *regularly*.

- Each person should give *proportionately*.

These points may help a congregation meet its budget, but they hardly do justice to the biblical concept of stewardship. Why?

First, no person can *give* anything to God. God is the Maker *and Owner* of all things. God *gives* people nothing. God *entrusts* people with abilities and goods.

Second, we share nothing. We merely *manage and distribute* what belongs to God.

Third, *all of life* is to be a giving, serving process.

A useful purpose would be served if people living on planet Earth could be taken to the vicinity of the moon, pointed back to planet Earth, and asked: "Where did that come from, and what are we doing on it?" In short, "In heaven's name, why on earth?" Only when we see things from this perspective do we begin to ask the questions that we need to ask.

This handbook is offered with the prayer that it will expand people's horizons concerning the nature and scope of biblical stewardship.

Harry Wendt

H.N. Wendt

Suggestions for Using This Manual

In Heaven's Name, Why on Earth? digs into biblical materials pertaining to the responsible Christian use of life in creation and history. It may be used for personal reading, or as the basis for a study course. The manual consists of two sections:

1. The Biblical Picture
2. Three resource items:

   a. *Ten Deadly Delusions*
   b. *Vision for Ministry and Mission*
   c. *The Jesus Chair*

****

Section 1 contains three study units. At the end of each unit are discussion questions for use in small or large groups.

The three units make use of 16 illustrations to present their message. These illustrations are available as a set in the form of full-color overhead transparencies. The transparencies can also be found in the transparency package that accompanies *The Divine Drama* materials distributed by Crossways International.

 In illus. 1B and some of the illustrations that follow, a visual symbol for God is used. It consists of a round circle: God is one, without beginning or end. Four arrows point out from the circle. The *arrows* remind us that God is always one who acts, and the key quality of God's actions is *love*. As the arrows go *out* from the circle, so God's love always goes *out* from God. God is like a great tank full of love, kindness and mercy—a tank whose faucet is always turned on and whose contents always flow out, but never run out.

Section 2: The materials **in this section only** may be photocopied for use as handouts.

1. Churches might ponder *Vision for Ministry and Mission* as they determine structures and goals.

2. The *Ten Deadly Delusions* spell out false notions that mislead pastors and laypeople as they establish structures and goals. It is suggested that pastors and teachers hand out the "delusions" to people in their class, and use the "answers" as resource materials for themselves as they help people respond to the questions.

3. *The Jesus Chair* suggests how families, churches, Christian schools and Christians generally might install a "Jesus Chair." It can help people think through the implications of living in Jesus' presence.

Section 1

Crossways International
Minneapolis, MN

Unit 1

The Plan
The Problem
The Solution

Crossways International
Minneapolis, MN

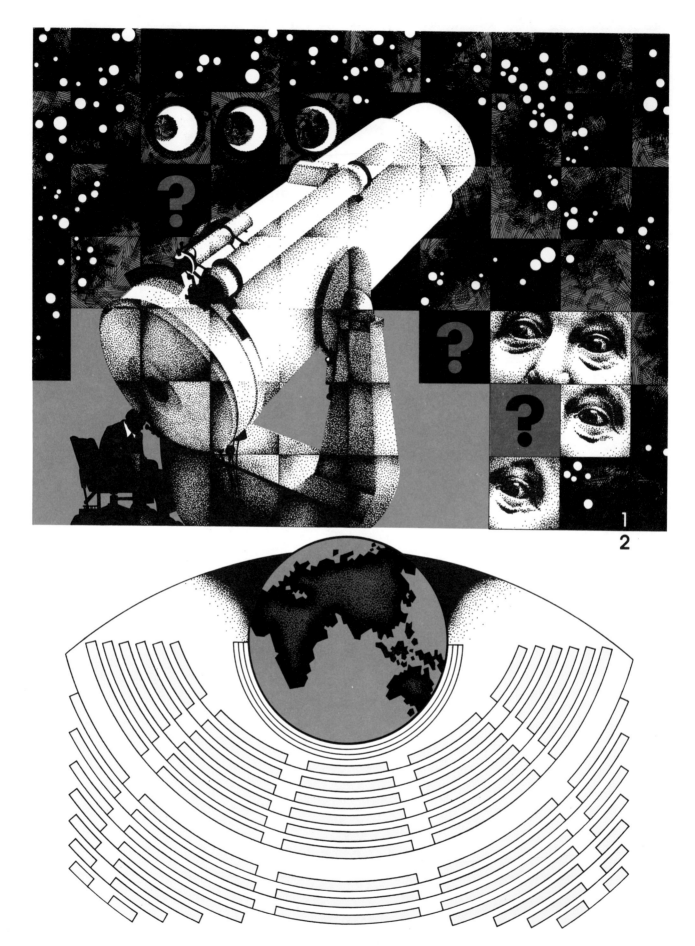

1A. FINDING GOD

1. **Illus. 1A-1** shows a person peering (*eyes*) through a telescope at a corner of a stylized universe, complete with phases of the moon. What he sees moves him to ask many questions (*question marks*).

2. How big is the universe? Technology enables astronauts in a space shuttle to orbit the equator at speeds up to 25,000 miles per hour. However, if people hope to get anywhere in the universe, they must travel at the speed of light, or seven times around the equator in one second. A few years ago, scientists said that even at that speed, it would take fourteen billion years to reach the limits of known space, which they said was only about 1/1,000,000,000th of theoretical space. Today some say that outer space is limitless.

3. When we look through a microscope, we see another incredible universe. Take the human body, for example. If we could join end-to-end all the veins, arteries and capillaries found in the average human body, they would reach from 2½ to 4 times around the equator. The fibers that make up the average human brain would reach to the moon and back. It we could flatten out the components that make up the large intestine, they would cover three football fields. If we could store all the information stored in the average human brain on 3½-inch computer disks, the pile of disks would be almost 6,000 miles high.

4. Though the things seen through telescopes and microscopes point to God's existence, they do not reveal God's identity and character.

5. We never find God; God is not lost. We are lost, and God finds us. The Bible reveals God as "the hound of heaven" who searches for people to draw them back into fellowship with God and with one another, Genesis 3:8,9; Luke 15:1–10.

6. **Illus. 1A-2** depicts an amphitheater, consisting of a stage and seats. The scenery on the stage is planet Earth, including the ancient Near East in which the biblical narrative unfolds. The illustration's message is: God is not just in the heavens. He is everywhere! Though telescopes and microscopes reveal God's footprints throughout creation, we must look elsewhere to discover something about God's heart, character and disposition. We must look to God's footprints in history.

7. The Bible teaches that God has seen fit to make tiny, fragile planet Earth the special stage for God's activities. God's footprints crisscross all history. These footprints provide answers to humanity's questions about life, death and eternity.

8. The biblical narrative indeed reveals God's divine drama. However, the more we study that drama, the more we learn that we do not merely watch it happen. We are all on stage, taking part in it—whether we realize it or not, whether we want to or not.

1B.   I BELIEVE IN GOD: MAKER, OWNER AND PROVIDER

1. Two words might well be added to the First Article of the Apostles' Creed: "I believe in God the Father Almighty, Maker *and Owner* of heaven and earth."

2. Illus. 1B depicts the truth implicit in this emended version of the First Article of the Apostles' Creed. The open hands are those of God, who made, owns, and provides for creation. God's "thumbs" are pressed into the sides of planet Earth, for the God who created the universe still owns it.

3. The figures within the world represent:

   a. *Head:* each person on planet Earth
   b. *Plate, knife and fork:* food
   c. *Dollar sign:* money
   d. *House:* people's dwellings
   e. *Large and small male and female figures:* human families
   f. *Ox:* possessions, means of making a living

4. How much do you pay for a loaf of bread? The price depends on what and where you buy. However, in reality we pay nothing for a loaf of bread, or anything else.

   a. When a farmer places a seed into soil, the seed he plants and the soil into which he places it are made and owned by God. God provides the sun and rain that give rise to the seed's fertilization and growth. In due course, one seed produces many seeds. Eventually the farmer harvests what God provides.

   b. When we purchase a loaf of bread, we do not pay for the bread as such. We merely return "service in a storable, exchangeable form" (money) to the farmer, trucker, flour miller, baker and storekeeper for producing the bread and making it available for purchase.

5. *The hands* in the lower center are inspired by Jesus' first beatitude, "Blessed are the poor in spirit, for theirs is the kingdom of heaven," Matthew 5:3. The first part of this statement might well be translated, "Blessed are they who know that they are beggars before God." Everything beggars receive comes to them freely from outside themselves. Similarly, God made and owns us. God provides. We receive, but never own. What beggars we are!

6. The figures in the lower right and left point to the response God desires from humanity. God wants us to:

   a. Thank and praise God (*figure with raised hands*), Psalm 103:5, 118:1.

   b. Serve and obey God (*figure in servant posture*), Psalm 110:1,2; Deuteronomy 6:4,5; Matthew 4:10.

© H.N. Wendt

1C.　THE ORIGINAL PLAN

1. Illus. 1C shows:

   a. The symbol for God, on which is a *crown*. God is King of the universe.

   b. A male and female figure with hands raised in praise to God. A double-headed arrow goes from each person to God and neighbor. A symbol of the commandments stands between the two persons. A symbol of each person in the servant posture is placed to the left and right of the persons. The message is that God wants us to live to serve God and others.

   c. Planet Earth, with the human family living in unity.

   d. A man's hand and a woman's hand joined in fellowship.

2. The illustration depicts God's original plan—that all should live together:

   a. under God as King,
   b. as one united family,
   c. with each asking, "How can I use life to glorify God by serving humanity?"

3. Whatever God asks us to believe and do is designed to equip us to:

   a. honor God,
   b. benefit others,
   c. experience a sense of worth,
   d. find real meaning in life, and
   e. create unity in the human family at local, national and international levels.

4. God never asks us to do anything for the sake of God's ego. God does not need us—we need God. God wants nothing but our well-being. Whatever God asks us to believe and do benefits *others—and us.*

5. We humans are to take good care of God's creation, which includes "our" bodies (which God still owns).

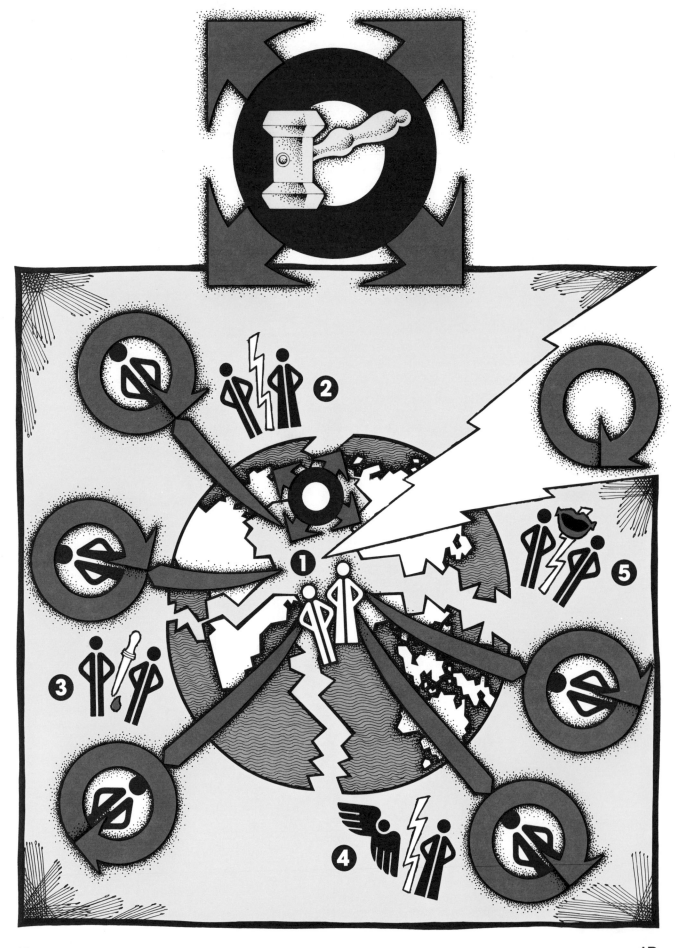

1D. THE PLAN DESTROYED

1. Genesis 2:4b–11:9 describes sin destroying God's original plan.

   a. Sin struck at the heart of the trust/obedience relationship between God and humanity.

   b. It tore the human scene apart at all levels, and corrupted the relationship between:

      (1) God and people, Genesis 2,3;
      (2) man and woman, Genesis 2,3;
      (3) brother and brother, Genesis 4,5;
      (4) the heavenly and the earthly, Genesis 6:1–4; chs. 6–9;
      (5) nation and nation, Genesis 10,11.

      (The numbers in 1b. correspond to those in the illustration.)

2. *Concern for community* has been replaced by the *curse of individualism*. Sin breaks the relationship between God and humanity, makes people prisoners to self (*person locked in circle*), and creates divisions between the sexes, in families and among the nations. Finally, it brings humanity under divine judgment (*gavel*).

3. Chaos manifests itself not merely in human relations, but also in the way people exploit God's created order for personal advantage rather than use it responsibly to the glory of God in the service of humanity.

© H.N. Wendt

1E. THE PLAN RESTORED

1. When sin disrupted God's good plan, God did not desert creation and humanity. God remained in fellowship with humanity, forgave humanity, and set about restoring creation and people to God's original plan.

2. Today some scientists suggest that "in the beginning" the universe was a ball of incredible energy as big an atom—and exploded! Within a fraction of a second the universe was formed. This theory is known as the "big bang" theory.

3. The Bible teaches that the God who created this vast universe and fills every corner of it, became like a seed within the womb of the Virgin Mary, and was born in the Person of Jesus the Messiah. Jesus walked on this dusty earth under the blue skies and breathed the air we breathe.

4. At Jesus' baptism, a voice from the cloud declared the nature of Jesus' Messiahship. It declared Jesus to be a Servant-King, Mark 1:9–11.

   a. *Crown:* The words "Thou art my beloved Son" are from Psalm 2:7, a royal psalm used when an heir from the line of David was anointed into office as king.

   b. *Servant figure with halo:* The words, "With Thee I am well pleased," are from Isaiah's first servant song, Isaiah 42:1–4; see v. 1. They declare that the Messiah that the people of God had been expecting for centuries came as a Servant King who summons His people to live as He does.

5. Jesus' people rejected Him, and the disciples let Him down badly. According to John's Gospel, Jesus took the disciples, the core of His new people, into an upper room. There He, their King, took a bowl of water and a towel and washed their feet, John 13:1–17 (*lower right corner*). Eventually the authorities crucified Him (*cross*). The disciples were confused and shattered. But, wonder of all wonders, three days later Jesus was alive again (*empty tomb*).

6. In the resurrection, the Father endorsed Jesus' Messiahship. In vindicating Jesus, the Father stated that there can be no attempt to get rid of Jesus again. Jesus is the Messiah, and the secret and wisdom of the universe.

7. Though the disciples failed Jesus miserably, He never once rebuked them after the resurrection. He appeared among them, declared His peace to them (John 20:19,21,26), served them breakfast on a seashore (John 21:12), asked them if they loved Him, and commanded them to follow Him, John 21:15–19. The answer to the world's problems lies in believing what Jesus says to us, and doing what He asks us to do.

8. Through faith in Jesus, people are restored to unity with God and each other.

QUESTIONS TO PONDER

1. The following statement appeared in a publication issued by St. Columba's Church, Hanover Park, Chicago:

   > If the whole world were a village of 1,000 people, only 60 would be Americans. All others would represent the rest of the world; 303 would be white, 330 Christian. Five hundred would be unable to read or write, and 800 would be constantly hungry and sickly. The 60 Americans would have one half the total income of the village and a life expectancy almost twice as long as the others. Of the 60 Americans, members of the lowest income group among them would be better off financially than the average of the remaining villagers. Can you imagine a community where 6% of the people have almost all of the food and wealth, and four-fifths of the people are hungry? This is the world community of which we are the wealthy part.

   What arguments do people use to rationalize ("rational-lies") why they need do little or nothing to help the world situation?

2. "God has been very good to us in this country. God has really blessed us and given us many wonderful things to enjoy." Evaluate this statement.

3. Mark, Merv, Megan and Molly play tennis (or bridge, golf, etc.) three mornings every week. They insist: "We enjoy it, and do it to the glory of God." Evaluate their actions and argument.

4. What yardstick does society at large use to measure "success" in life? What yardstick does Jesus use? How do the two yardsticks differ? What yardstick do you use to determine success?

5. "We are not here to live comfortably; we are here to live usefully." Why is it so important for Christians to understand this, and act on it?

6. Edward Gibbon, in his "The Decline and Fall of the Roman Empire," suggests as the five major reasons for the collapse of the Roman Empire the following:

   (1) Family life disintegrated.
   (2) Traditional ethical systems were ignored.
   (3) Entertainment became perverse and immoral.
   (4) Vast amounts were spent on maintaining the military machine to defend the Empire.
   (5) The Empire's economy collapsed.

   What can we learn from this? What steps do you plan to take in your personal, family and church life to help reverse similar trends in today's society?

Unit 2

Priorities? No!
Options? Yes!

Crossways International
Minneapolis, MN

2A. CHRISTIANITY: AN IMPORTANT PART OF LIFE? THE MOST IMPORTANT PART OF LIFE? OR WHAT?

1. In the lower left corner of illus. 2A is a person (let's call him Sylvester) who is puzzled.

2. Sylvester is looking at the world around him (*symbolized by the circle*) and trying to work out how everything fits together. Above all, he is wondering how Christianity (*symbolized by the church and Bible*) fits into all those other things that make demands on his time.

3. The following clamor for attention in Sylvester's world:

   a. *Dome:* government
   b. *Diplomas:* education
   c. *Plate, knife and fork:* food
   d. *Parents with children:* family
   e. *Dollar sign:* making, using and saving money
   f. *Baseball:* leisure activities
   g. *Factory:* work

4. Sylvester is asking, "How do I fit Christianity into all these other things?"

5. Sylvester is asking the wrong question. He should be asking, "How do I fit all these other things into Christianity?"

6. Many people think of Christianity as an *important part* of life, even as the *most important part* of life. However, Jesus is to be Lord of *all* life, not just *part* of it.

7. The reason for the confusion usually flows from an incorrect understanding of Jesus' words in Matthew 6:33, where Jesus says, "But strive *first* for the kingdom of God and His righteousness, and all these things will be given to you as well." However, in Luke's version of this passage (12:31), Jesus says, "Instead, strive for His kingdom, and these things will be given to you as well." (Note: No *first*!)

8. The context in both cases makes clear Jesus' meaning. He tells His followers they are not to fritter away life worrying about what they will eat, drink and wear. He says it is God's business to worry about such things, and to provide them with what God knows they need. After all, the God who provides a person with a body will provide clothes to cover that body, and the God who endows a person with life will provide food to sustain that life. What Matthew says in a Jewish way ("first") Luke says in a Gentile (non-Jewish) way.

9. In Matthew 4:10, Jesus says, "Worship the Lord your God, and serve *only* Him."

10. In short, we are here to devote all life to the service of God and others. God does not seek *first* place in our lives, but the *only* place!

Sylvester now looks much happier. He has sorted a few things out in his mind. He now knows that Jesus must be at the center of all his believing, thinking, speaking, and doing. The Christian faith gives direction to everything in life.

1. *Government:* It is essential to have some kind of government at local, national and international levels. Without it, chaos prevails. Good governments help people live together meaningfully, and to serve and care for each other responsibly in community.

2. *Education:* God wants people to develop their minds and skills. A God-pleasing education helps equip people to use life in a way that is personally satisfying and useful to others.

3. *Plate, knife and fork:* People need to eat healthy food to function properly and to be an asset in the service of others. Those who neglect their health run the risk of becoming a liability others must serve.

4. *Parents with children:* The first several commandments talk about our duties to God; those that follow talk about our duties to others. In the second group the importance of establishing a healthy family life is first on the list. The family is the basic unit in society. Parents exercise a tremendous influence on their children—whether they believe it or not, whether they try to do so or not.

5. *Dollar sign:* Money plays a key role in keeping the wheels turning in everyday life. Money is stored service, stored servanthood. It is to be used to glorify God by serving others.

6. *Baseball:* People need leisure time to re-create (hence, "recreation") their bodies and minds. Lack of fitness dulls the mind, endangers health, and makes people less useful in the service of others.

7. *Factory:* God wants people to work to render service to others in the community. Some people work to produce *goods* people need. Others work to provide *services* people need.

2C.   GOD'S CHURCH

1. What is the first thought that enters your mind when you hear the word "church"? A building? Worship? Bible? Organ? Choir? Money? Pastor?

2. Because of the way the organized church operates in Western society, the first word that comes into many minds is "building." However, the Bible never uses the word "church" in the sense of a building. A building is a *facility*. God's church is made up of *people*.

3. Illus. 2C depicts what the New Testament means when it speaks of God's "church." It shows God's world. The symbol for God is in the center. Superimposed on it are symbols of the Servant Christ, the crucifixion and the empty tomb. It also contains six circles. Five of the circles contain symbols depicting the following vocations (*beginning at top left*): janitor, chemist, musician, engineer, farmer.

4. God calls the Church, God's people, into existence through His empowering word of grace. God teaches them who God is, what God has made and owns, what God has done through Jesus for their redemption. God then sends them back to live to His praise and glory (*raised hands*) by serving others in a Christlike manner.

5. The arrows have two heads. They point in and out, indicating that God's people are the summoned and the sent, the called and the commissioned, the gathered and the scattered.

6. All worship facilities should have two prominent signs on them. Above the entrance door there should be a sign saying, "Servants' Entrance." Above the exit door there should be a sign saying, "Your Mission Field Ahead."

7. The circle in the top right of the illustration is empty. In it, sketch a symbol of your vocation, and consider how you can carry it out to the glory of God and in the service of people.

2D.   SATAN'S CHURCH

1. The word "secular" is derived from a Latin word that refers to things of this world and age. In Western society, the word is applied to those areas of life and activity in the world that, theoretically, have no direct relationship with God.

2. Accordingly, people speak of "spiritual interests" (things connected with "religion") and "secular interests" (things not connected with "religion").

3. It is wrong and dangerous to look at things this way. There is no secular realm. The sphere of life alternate to the *spiritual* ("Spirit"-ual, "led by the Spirit") is the *satanic,* 1 John 3:8; Matthew 6:24; Romans 8:12–14.

4. Illus. 2D builds on illus. 2C. Satan is at the center of life, framed in the arrow for sin, self-centeredness and self-service. The arms of the persons in the circles are not raised in praise to God, but reflect an attitude of indifference to God.

5. There is one created order. God made it. God owns it. Either God controls events in the lives of all who live on planet Earth, or Satan does.

6. Martin Luther suggests that we think of ourselves as a horse, with someone sitting in the saddle to direct us. There are only two riders: God or Satan. The question is, "Who sits in the saddle of my life?" C.S. Lewis wrote: "There is no neutral ground in the universe. Every square inch is claimed by God and counter-claimed by Satan."

7. When we take this matter seriously, we find ourselves involved in a struggle; Satan does not want to give up control of our lives. The presence of this struggle need not perturb us; its absence should. Its presence indicates that our faith is alive and that we are fighting a genuine warfare against the Satanic realm, Ephesians 6:10–18.

8. It follows that every person on the face of planet Earth serves, worships, witnesses to, and supports the work of either God or Satan at every step in life. These are the only options. There is no escape from being involved in the struggle.

2E.   THE BODY OF CHRIST

A.   THE HUMAN BODY

1. Do the following:

   a. Raise your right arm parallel to the floor.

   b. Raise your right thumb and wriggle it.

   c. Try to scratch your right thumb with your right thumb (see 2.d. below).

2. How does the body operate?

   a. It contains a variety of organs and members. The brain directs their movements.

   b. Though some of the body's members are visible and prominent, many others are not, but none complains about not being in the limelight on center stage.

   c. When one part of the body is injured, the rest of the body does not cut it off or out. It hurts with it, heals it, and compensates until it is restored to health.

   d. No member of the human body can serve itself.

B.   CHRIST'S BODY—THE CHURCH

1. Paul refers to the church as "the body of Christ," Romans 12:1–8; 1 Corinthians 12; Ephesians 1:22,23; Colossians 2:19.

2. Some understand the term to refer to a local congregation as a group, a community of people. However, the term says more than that. It describes how God's people are to function in community.

   a. The local church is a community of people possessing skills and abilities for use in a wide range of occupations and situations (illus. 2E, symbols with "body").

   b. "Members" of the "body" are to get their directions about what they should believe and do from Jesus, "the Head," who communicates with them through His Word (note the Bible in Jesus' "Head") and sacraments.

   c. Each "member" is to become more and more what Jesus wants, and then use life to help other members within the "body" become what Jesus wants. When one member is spiritually or physically weak or troubled, other members render support, help and healing.

   d. Jesus' "body" acts for Jesus to draw others into "member"-ship with it. It is Jesus' incarnate extension to the world. It is to act *for* Jesus, *as* Jesus, *to* Jesus, Matthew 25:40.

3. There is no such thing as "private" Christianity. *Personal* faith, yes! *Private* faith, never! Discipleship is always lived out in community.

QUESTIONS TO PONDER

1. Discuss the validity of the following two statements:

   a. "Christians should not meddle in politics; they have better things to do."
   b. "Business is one thing—religion is another; they should not be mixed."

2. "I really enjoy going to church. I may not make it every Sunday, but I go when I can. My church life means a lot to me!"

   What view of Christianity does the above statement reflect?

3. What are the implications of the following statements for the life of a Christian?

   a. "Christians are not merely *to go to church*; they are *to be God's church* in the world."
   b. "Christians are not merely *to support* missions; they are *to be God's mission* to the world."

4. One of the major goals of the demonic realm is to sidetrack people from living to be servants of others. What tools and arguments does the demonic use in seeking to achieve this goal?

5. In Matthew 25:14–30 Jesus teaches us that if He gives certain people "five measures" of ability and opportunity, He expects them to produce "five measures" of achievement in the service of others—and if two, then two; if one, then one.

   How does Jesus' view of things differ from the views of society at large?

6. Deuteronomy 8:1–10 is often read at Thanksgiving services in churches. However, 8:1–10 should not be separated from 8:11–20.

   a. Why?
   b. What does God say to nations, communities and individuals in 8:1–20?

7. History teaches us that no nation survives for long after it has acquired wealth and access to considerable amounts of leisure time. Why is this so?

8. After Sultan Ibn al Saud of Saudi Arabia accompanied American astronauts on a space mission some years ago, he wrote, "The first day we pointed to our countries, the second day to our continents, and the third day to Planet Earth."

   What did he mean, and what might we learn from his comments?

Unit 3

Managing Me
Managing Money

Crossways International
Minneapolis, MN

BECAUSE

THEREFORE

3A. OBEDIENCE: WHY AND HOW?

1. Some believe that, in the Old Testament, people tried to save themselves *by keeping God's laws*. When God saw that did not work out, God changed the approach—with the result that God now saves New Testament people *by grace*. The truth is that, since the fall of Adam, people have always been saved by grace.

2. Throughout both the Old and New Testaments, God invariably first tells God's people what God has done for them, and then indicates how they are to respond. The order is always, "*Because I*, God, have done this for you—*therefore you*, My people, are to do this for Me and others," Deuteronomy 5:15; 16:12; 24:18,22. Ephesians chs. 1–3 constitute a "Because"; Ephesians 4:1 begins a lengthy "Therefore."

3. The upper section of illus. 3A (BECAUSE) has two sections. The left section depicts the Exodus-Sinai-wilderness events. The right section depicts Jesus' servant life, crucifixion, death, burial and resurrection. In Luke 9:31, these events are referred to as Jesus' "exodus" (saving event), which He will "complete" in Jerusalem.

4. The lower section of illus. 3A (THEREFORE) depicts the response God has sought from humanity throughout history. God's will is that people serve God and others. In Ephesians 2:8–10, Paul establishes the following order: by grace, through faith, for works (*better:* for service).

5. Human nature wishes to reverse the divine order. People by nature think, "If I do good things (BECAUSE), God will forgive me (THEREFORE). To think this way is to deny the grace of God and to destroy the salvation process.

3B. CARING FOR OURSELVES TO GIVE OURSELVES

1. God made us. God owns us. God endows us with abilities. God wants us to care for and develop ourselves so that God might use us as God's instruments in the service of others. Illus. 3B depicts a person surrounded by four segments representing volitional, emotional, physical and intellectual powers.

2. What is involved in caring for, and developing, oneself? Jesus says, "You shall love the Lord your God with all your heart, and with all your soul, and with all your strength, and with all your mind," Mark 12:30,31.

3. "With all your heart" (*top left segment*): This really means, "with all your will." God wants us to have an informed will (*law-code*) equipped to weigh up moral issues (*scales*). As with a traffic light, God wants us to know when not to proceed (*red*), when to proceed with caution (*amber*), and when to proceed with a good conscience (*green*).

4. "With all your soul" (*upper right segment*): Our external demeanor reflects our inner disposition. God wants us to develop a Christ-like demeanor that attracts others to us, equips us to serve them, and creates unity in the community.

5. "With all your strength" (*lower right segment*): God wants us to eat and drink responsibly, and exercise to keep fit. When we do that, our bodies are more likely to be instruments God can use to serve others, rather than liabilities others must serve.

6. "With all your mind" (*lower left segment*): God wants us to read, watch, and study things that will edify us, and equip us to serve others better.

7. "Thou shalt love thy neighbor as thyself" does not mean "50% for others and 50% for me." God wants us to devote life 100% to serving Him through serving others. Our goal is to become more what God intended us to be. The more we do that, the more God can use us to help others become what God intended them to be.

8. God writes the agenda for our actions. We serve others as God wants us to serve them—not as we want to serve them, or as they want to be served.

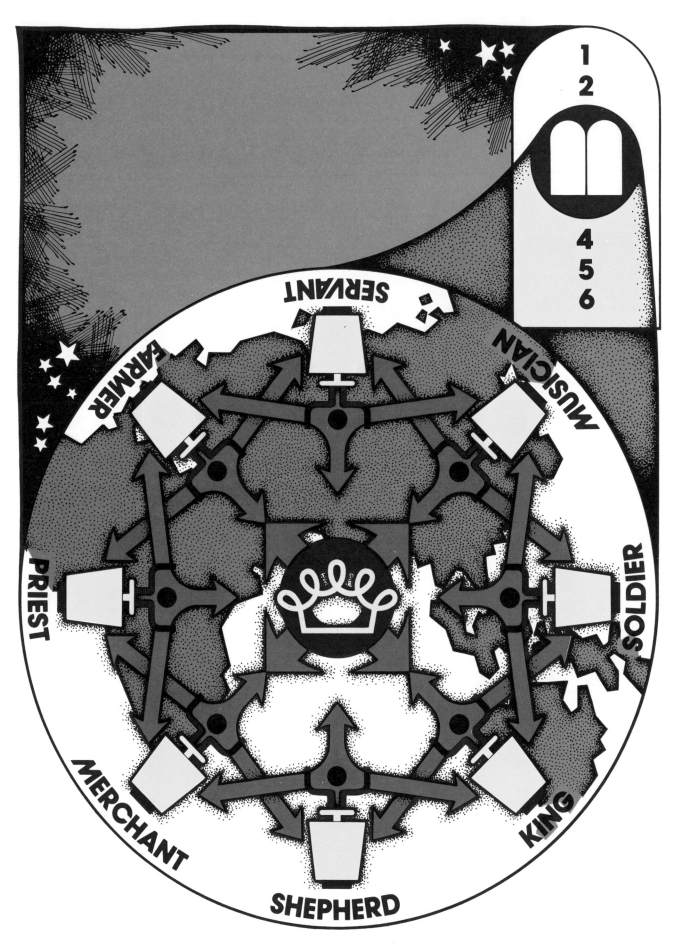

SERVANT

FARMER

MUSICIAN

PRIEST

SOLDIER

MERCHANT

KING

SHEPHERD

1
2

4
5
6

3C

3C. GOD'S PEOPLE: A KINGDOM OF PRIESTS

A.   THE PRIESTHOOD DEFINED

1. After God gathered ancient Israel around God's presence at Sinai, God said to them, "The whole earth is mine, but you shall be for me a priestly kingdom and a holy nation," Exodus 19:5b,6. God then made a covenant with them, Exodus 20.

2. In referring to them as a "priestly kingdom," God did not mean that they were to do nothing but perform rituals in the Temple. They were to live under God as their "King," and serve God as "priests."

3. In this context, what is meant by the term "priest"? A priest is a person who:

    (a) handles "sacred things," and
    (b) goes to God for others and to others for God.

4. What are "sacred things"? God says, "The whole earth is mine." Everything we touch has a sacred quality about it, for God made and owns all things.

5. A Christian "priest" uses creation and life to glorify God and serve others.

B.   THE PRIESTHOOD DEMONSTRATED

1. The main section of illus. 3C depicts planet Earth with the symbol for God superimposed on it. God made and owns planet Earth; God is King of creation (*crown*).

2. Around God is a circle of *eight pulpits*. A person stands in each, with arms raised in praise. All Christians, no matter what their calling, are in a sacred situation before God. Furthermore, all Christians are to honor God by serving those around them (*arrows going from each person to God and others*).

3. In the upper right corner of illus. 3C is a symbol of the Sinai covenant. The numbers point to its structure. The first three are:

    (1) *Preamble:* "I am the Lord your God," Exodus 20:2.
    (2) *Historical Prologue:* "Who brought you out of the land of Egypt, out of the house of slavery," Exodus 20:2.
    (3) *Stipulations:* Commandments, Exodus 20:3–17.

4. The commandments given at Sinai served as guidelines to God's people for copying God's previous actions toward them, for living in community, and for living as a "priestly kingdom." Obedience brought honor to God, and well-being and happiness to the community. It also served as a magnet to attract other nations to God, Deuteronomy 4:6–8.

5. Though Christians today pursue many occupations, each Christian is to do everything as a royal priest of God, 1 Peter 2:8,9.

3D

3D. MONEY

1. *Illus. 3D-1:* Mary, whose hand is on the left, grows apples. Mark, on the right, makes wheels for wheelbarrows. One day Mary gives Mark a barrow load of apples, and he gives her a new wheel for her barrow. What are they "giving" each other? Nothing. Though Mary put effort into growing them, the apples belong to God. Though Mark put effort into making the wheel, the materials and skills he used belong to God.

2. *Illus. 3D-2:* In the final analysis, Mary and Mark exchange only the *effort* that went into producing the barrow load of apples and the wheel. It is easier to see the apples as a gift of God rather than the wheel. However, every manufactured article might well bear this label: "Raw materials—property of God; final product—fashioned by people using ingenuity and strength supplied by God."

3. *Illus. 3D-3:* Perhaps one day Mary needs a wheel for her barrow, but Mark does not need a barrow load of apples. Mary now gives him Christian effort, love and service in a storable, exchangeable form: money. Money, then, is effort in a form that can be stored, exchanged and put to work. Money is stored servanthood.

4. Money in itself is a neutral, lifeless thing—neither good nor bad. Even so, its use poses challenges and dangers. In 1 Timothy 6:6–10, Paul writes:

   > Of course, there is great gain in godliness combined with contentment; for we brought nothing into the world, so that we can take nothing out of it; but if we have food and clothing, we will be content with these. But those who want to be rich fall into temptation and are trapped by many senseless and harmful desires that plunge people into ruin and destruction. For *the love of money* [emphasis added] is a root of all kinds of evil, and in their eagerness to be rich some have wandered away from the faith and pierced themselves with many pains.

   Hence, not *money*, but the *love of money* is the root of all evils.

5. In 1 Corinthians 10:31, Paul writes, "So, whether you eat or drink, or whatever you do, do everything for the glory of God." To determine the divine validity of everything they do, Christians are to ask, "Will my actions ultimately glorify God and benefit others? In what way?"

3E. PLAYING WITH PERCENTAGES

A. THE WRONG APPROACH (*Illus. 3E-1*)

1. These days, many people are bombarded with requests to give of their time, talents and treasure ("three T's") to help countless needy causes. How much should we "give" of our "three T's"?

2. Sylvester assumes that those "three T's" are all his, and that he must decide what percentage he will give to God of what is his, of what God has given him. No doubt, he assumes that after he has given his fair share to God, the rest is his to do with as he pleases.

B. THE RIGHT APPROACH (*Illus. 3E-2*)

1. We own nothing. God made and continues to own everything, including "our" bodies, Exodus 19:5; Haggai 2:8; 1 Corinthians 4:7; Psalm 100; Deuteronomy 8.

2. Sylvester must change his question to, "How much of what belongs to God do I need to keep and use for my own needs?"

3. We do not own God's creation; we merely manage it. Hence, Christians should not speak of Christian *giving*, but of Christian *management* and Christian *distribution*.

4. The principle set forth above applies to all of life—not just to life in the organized church. The Kingdom of God embraces all of life; the traditional division of life into spiritual and secular realms is invalid.

5. When the Macedonian Christians were considering what to make available for the support of the needy in Jerusalem, "they gave themselves first to the Lord," 2 Corinthians 8:5. Only after people have done this are they in a condition to grapple with what the Bible has to say about the use of the material order.

6. When John Wesley, the founder of the Methodist Church, first became a Christian, his salary was 30 pounds per year. He lived on 28 and made two available to the church. When his salary increased to 50, he lived on 28 and made 22 available to the church. When it increased to 100, he lived on 28 and made 72 available to the church. The message of the "Wesley Way" for today is clear and challenging.

3F.   THE APPROPRIATE OFFERING

1. The Old Testament prophets repeatedly attacked the Israelites for thinking they could keep God happy if they covered up their shallow obedience by offering God an abundance of animals in sacrifice, Hosea 6:6, Micah 6:6–8. During His ministry, Jesus attacked many who adopted a similar attitude, Matthew 9:13.

2. Paul reminds Christians what their lifelong sacrifice must be:

> I appeal to you therefore, brothers and sisters, by the mercies of God, to present
> your bodies as a living sacrifice, holy and acceptable to God.
> *— Romans 12:1*

3. Jesus sacrificed Himself for us by giving His life away on a cross. Jesus summons us to offer our bodies as a living sacrifice, not to the flames as burnt offerings, but to Him through the service of others. Jesus wants us to do this, not just for an hour or so on a Sunday morning, but throughout life.

4. Paul writes:

> Christ died for all, so that those who live might no longer live for themselves, but
> for him who died and was raised for them.
> *— 2 Corinthians 5:15*

1. A Chinese proverb states:

    > When a butterfly flaps its wings in China, it affects the weather patterns around
    > planet Earth.

    What does the proverb mean, and what light does it throw on biblical teaching about the corporate nature of Christian discipleship?

2. Which of the following three statements is biblically acceptable, and why?

    a. "I am to serve others as they want me to serve them."
    b. "I am to serve others as I feel disposed to serve them."
    c. "I am to serve others as God wants me to serve them."

3. "There are many worthy causes to which people should contribute. However, it is important that they give first to God's work, to the work of the Church."

    Evaluate this statement.

4. Note point 4 on page 35, and read 1 Timothy 6:6–10 carefully.

    a. How seriously does society take this passage today?
    b. What price does it pay for ignoring it?

5. Early in the nineties, a major church body numbering three million members made a special effort to raise funds for World Relief. The result: $3,000,000, or $1 per member.

    a. How much do you (and your family) spend each month on eating out? How much do you give each month to help work among the truly needy?
    b. What does the comparison reveal about your commitment to local, national and international social justice?

6. Have another look at illus. 3E, and read the comments concerning John Wesley's actions in point 6 on page 37. If Wesley's example were followed today, what major (but exciting) problem would face the church?

Section 2

Crossways International
Minneapolis, MN

VISION FOR MISSION AND MINISTRY

We, the members of _____ Church are a privileged community of people who, by the grace of God in Jesus the Messiah, may call ourselves sons and daughters of God the Father and brothers and sisters of Jesus the Messiah. We live on, and use, a planet that our Heavenly Father made and owns. Similarly, we use bodies, skills and resources that our Heavenly Father made and owns. By virtue of the Holy Spirit's work through the means of grace (Word and sacraments), in faith we lay hold of Jesus the Messiah—crucified, risen, present and finally to reappear—as Savior and Lord. With joy, we trust in the forgiveness of sins our Lord and Brother, Jesus the Messiah, won for us at the cross, and has richly and freely lavished on us. With awe, we seek to walk through life the way our Lord walked, using creation as God the Father would have us use it, and using life totally to serve our God by serving the needs of humanity about us.

We, the members of _____ Church, are a responsible people. We acknowledge that we are all called to fulfill the above mission and ministry. Though we employ certain persons to serve in a full-time capacity within the organized congregation, they are placed over and among us by God to equip us for our own full-time ministries.

However, we, the members of _____ Church, are also a realistic people. We know that though the final victory, assuring us of our eternal salvation, was declared at the empty tomb, there is no neutral ground in the Universe. Every square inch of creation, and every minute of time, is claimed by God and counter-claimed by Satan. Hence, we pledge ourselves, as those redeemed by the blood of Jesus the Messiah, to walk in a way worthy of our high calling in Jesus the Messiah and to fight a God-pleasing battle against the powers of evil and darkness in and around us. We seek to do this by:

1. Praising God through a diversity of edifying worship and expressive music. (Worship)

2. Praying that we might honor the God and Father of our Lord, Jesus the Messiah, at all times and in all ways, and serve as instruments to resolve the problems we lay at His feet. (Prayer)

3. Providing opportunities for people of all ages to grow in the knowledge of the written Word, and urging them to participate in what is offered, that they might believe and follow the Living Word as informed, committed disciples. (Education)

4. Proclaiming the message of the Kingdom of God to the world, inviting people into that Kingdom through the forgiveness of sins, and assimilating and nurturing those people whom the Holy Spirit gathers into His and our Church family, at home and abroad. (Evangelism, Missions)

5. Managing and sharing the material resources that God makes available to us in a manner that reflects the attitude of Jesus the Messiah toward His Father and the created order. We understand ourselves to be managers of God's creation, called to distribute responsibly what God has placed at our disposal for the benefit of all. We shall not ask, "How much of that which is mine will I give to God?" but, "How much of that which is God's will I keep for my own needs?" (Stewardship of Material Goods)

6. Helping couples understand and practice the promises they made to each other in their marriage vows, and equipping them to fulfil their God-given responsibility to teach the Christian faith to their children and to train them to walk in the ways of Jesus the Messiah. (Marriage and Family Life)

7. Promoting the development of edifying relationships and meaningful ministries in and through small groups. (Nurture and Support Groups)

8. Rejoicing with those who rejoice, sharing the sorrows of the suffering, encouraging those enduring trials, and supplying the needs of those around the world who are burdened by any need of body, soul or spirit. (Caring Discipleship)

9. Equipping all members of _____ Church to imitate Jesus the Messiah as responsible stewards of God's creation and concerned servants of God and humanity in all they do—in the congregation, in their homes, in their daily work, and in the community, the nation and the world. (The Priesthood of All Believers in the Totality of Life)

In the light of the above, we, the members of _____ Church pledge that we shall never judge the success of our efforts in terms of the size of any buildings we possess or erect, or by the numbers we attract into those buildings, or by the facilities we install in those buildings, or by the number of programs we run within their walls. We pledge that we shall always remember that God alone determines the success of our efforts in terms of the changes He sees in our lives and by the changes He empowers us to effect in the lives of others, both within and beyond our congregation. To God alone be the glory!

Slogan: A Changed People Changing Lives In a Changing World

THE TEN DEADLY DELUSIONS

Down through the centuries, the Church has spoken and written about what it calls *The Seven Deadly Sins*. Perhaps the 20th-century Church needs to think about the following *Ten Deadly Delusions* that many within its ranks embrace. What is wrong or misleading about each statement? How might the thought-pattern behind each delusion hinder or cripple the worldwide mission of the Church?

Delusion 1: "God wants us to give Him a percentage of what He has first given us. If only people would practice tithing!"

Delusion 2: "God has blessed us in this country with many wonderful things to enjoy."

Delusion 3: "This country offers many opportunities for people to achieve success for themselves."

Delusion 4: "We must put God first in our lives. Christianity must always be the most important part of life!"

Delusion 5: "We are to serve God in the secular realm as well as in the spiritual sphere."

Delusion 6: "We must continue to stress the importance of grace, and preach the gospel of the forgiveness of sins with power!"

Delusion 7: "We must meet our own budget before we send anything to outside causes."

Delusion 8: "With all the troubles now plaguing the nation, we need to train as many professional church workers as possible."

Delusion 9: "It is good to see that the Church is now organizing 'servant events' for young people. There should be more of them!"

Delusion 10: "It seems that other countries put more emphasis on the importance of the *community*. Because we in the United States put more emphasis on the importance of the *individual*, we have more freedom here."

Answers to: "The Ten Deadly Delusions."

1. God gives us nothing; God retains ownership of creation. The First Article of the Creed might well be edited to read, "I believe in God the Father Almighty, Maker *and Owner* of heaven and earth." There is no such thing as Christian giving. There is only *Christian management*, and *Christian distribution*. The problem in the church is not Christian giving; it is un-Christian keeping. The problem is not the high cost of living, but the cost of high living. God did not give humanity ownership of creation, but "dominion over" creation, Genesis 1:26.

   The practice of tithing is based on Old Testament principles. It can lead to confusion regarding what constitutes discipleship. For example, let's say Mr. A. earns $20,000 per year and gives $2,000. He has $18,000 left. Mr B. earns $100,000, gives $10,000, and has $90,000 over. Does Mr B. need $90,000 per year? If the response is that as we earn more, we increase our standard of living—a costly affair—then we do well to note the example of John Wesley, the father of Methodism. Wesley became a Christian while teaching at Oxford University in England. His salary was 30 pounds per year. He lived on 28 and gave 2. When his salary was increased to 50 pounds per year, he lived on 28 and gave 22. When his salary was increased to 100 pounds per year, he lived on 28 and gave 72. The "Wesley Way" is worthy of thought in a world in which the motto is, "Make what you can, can what you make, and sit on the lid." Wesley taught his followers that they should make as much as possible, save as much as possible, and give as much as possible. Money is merely stored service, "stored self," that facilitates service to others by proxy.

2. We do well to note the words of the first-century Roman satirist, Juvenal, who wrote, "Luxury is more ruthless than war." Note also John Calvin's comment, "The human mind is an idol factory." We are neither deserving nor special. God has not *blessed* us but *endowed* us. We are not here to live comfortably, but *usefully* —to use whatever God provides by serving others without limit in their every need, whoever or wherever they may be. Needs abound. We live in a world in which 6% of the people receive half the income, 50% are constantly hungry, 60% live in shanty-towns, and 70% are illiterate.

3. Success is not determined by what we accumulate for ourselves, but by what we do to the glory of God in the service of others, Matthew 25:31–46. The "Great American (or Australian or Western World) Dream" is proving to be a great nightmare in many frightening ways. Simply put, we are not here to accumulate riches, but to seek after righteousness.

4. God commands us to put Him *only*, not *first*, Matthew 4:10. Compare Matthew 6:33 with Luke 12:31 where the word "first" is omitted. To put God *first* is to operate with priorities. To put God *only* is to operate with options. Luther reminds us that each person is like a horse with a saddle, in which either Jesus or Satan holds the reins. C.S. Lewis said, "There is no neutral ground in the universe. Every square inch is claimed by God and counter-claimed by Satan." Christianity is not the most important part of life; Jesus calls us to full-time, not part-time, discipleship.

5. There is no secular realm (see 4. above). There is one world that God made and owns. We use life and creation either according to God's will, or according to the will of the devil, the world and our flesh (Luther). We would do well to edit the Third Article of the Apostles' Creed so that it reads, "I believe in the Holy Spirit, the holy Christian Church, the communion of saints—*and I believe in the existence of the unholy Satanic Spirit, and the unholy demonic realm....*" The demonic is every person, power or influence that sidetracks us from living as servants of God and others, into living merely for ourselves.

46

6. True, but the "good news" of the New Testament is that the Messianic Age has broken in—with all that implies; see Isaiah 60; 61:1–7; Mark 1:1; John 20:30,31. We must beware of merely telling people why they should not do "good works" for the *wrong* reason, while failing to tell them what good works they should be doing for the *right* reason. Preaching the gospel and administering the sacraments is merely a means to an end—an end that the Anglican Catechism sums up beautifully: "The mission of the church is to restore all people to unity with God and each other, in Christ." Above the entrance doors of our churches we need a sign saying, "Servants' Entrance." Above the exit doors we need another sign saying, "Mission Field Ahead."

7. Though it is easy to criticize what some people in the Head Office might want to do with our benevolence, these people have seen something of the nightmares and challenges that exist beyond our own shores. True, local congregations need to remain financially viable. However, some tend to become slaves to their own facility. They provide amenities, fixtures and programs that everyone will enjoy, but do not weep for a heartbreaking world about which they know so little.

8. The answer is not merely a matter of training "professional church workers." To begin with, every Christian is called to be a priest of God. Whatever we touch has a sacred quality to it—for God made and owns all things. Hence, as priests of God, we constantly touch and handle sacred things. As a priest is one who goes to God for others and to others for God, so we, in our daily work, do something for God in the service of others. Those who preach sermons from pulpits are not doing something more sacred than those who paint houses or grow corn. Though there are differences in function, there are no degrees of holiness in the things God's people do. Luther wrote that the works of monks and priests "in God's sight is in no way superior to the works of a farmer laboring in the fields, or a woman scrubbing floors in her home." The view that scrubbing floors held as much dignity as occupying the pulpit radically changed the work ethic of Luther's day, and has made an impact on the world ever since. Furthermore, clergy are not so much professionals as those called by God to make a profession and to make it with a passion. If anything, their task is to equip God's priests for their work throughout creation, and to be protesters against the prevailing sin and corruption within society at large. Churches that have installed a number of professional workers can give the impression that those workers can assume full responsibility for the work of the Church, especially for the Christian nurture of the congregation's children and youth. This is a disastrous impression to give. Parents are God's children-workers and youth-workers!

9. For Christians, life itself is to be a servant event! We need to insert into the Second Article of the Creed, "...born of the Virgin Mary, *walked the way of a Servant without limit*, suffered....the third day He rose again from the dead, *He has not withdrawn but transformed His presence, makes Himself available in many distressing disguises that people might serve Him, and will at the Last Day finally reappear*, to judge the living and the dead *with reference to whether or not they have responded to His forgiving mercy by serving Him in those distressing disguises*."

10. There is no such thing as private Christianity. We are called to personal faith, yes—but never to private faith. It might be argued that the emphasis on individualism in the United States is destroying the fabric of its society. Christians are not free to do their *own thing*, but free (from the guilt, power and punishment of sin) to do *God's thing* by serving others. Free grace calls us to costly discipleship. In determining whether or not a certain action or lifestyle is God-pleasing, a person must ask: "If everyone were to do what I want to do, or pursue the lifestyle I plan to pursue, what would happen to the human race?" If the answer is that it would harm or destroy the human race, then no person has a right before God to do that deed or pursue that lifestyle.

THE JESUS CHAIR

In communicating the nature of Christian discipleship, a useful purpose can be served by placing a chair somewhere in the church sanctuary and labeling it "The Jesus Chair." Its significance can be explained as follows:

1. When Jesus was conceived by the Holy Spirit of the Virgin Mary, that which is fully God united itself with that which is fully human—though without sin. In other words, though the Second Person of the Trinity has always been God (divine nature), at the virginal conception that Person took into Himself a human nature.

2. From the moment of the conception until the moment immediately preceding the resurrection, Jesus did not always nor fully use His power as God. But from the moment of the resurrection onwards, He did always and fully use His power as God. From that moment onwards, for example, He filled the universe not merely as God, but also as man.

3. Beyond the resurrection, Jesus paid the disciples a series of "visible visits" to assure them that He was still with and among them. In ascending, Jesus stated, "There will be no more little visible visits, but I am not going away." The cloud into which He went (Acts 1:9) was a symbol of the divine presence.

4. The Apostles' Creed speaks of Jesus ascending into heaven and sitting at the right hand of the Father. However, in the ascension Jesus did not *withdraw* His presence, but *transformed* it. Furthermore, the Father does not have a right hand. The reference to Jesus sitting at the Father's right hand has to do with *authority,* not *locality.*

5. Jesus will remain among us until He reappears at the end of history. We Christians, therefore, live before Jesus' eyes. While we wait for Him to reappear, Jesus calls us to reflect His manner of life in our own lives. In short, we are to seek to make the invisible Jesus visible. Furthermore, our manner of life is not determined by the law codes of the Old Testament, but by Jesus' statement, "I give you a new commandment, that you love one another. Just as I have loved you, you also should love one another," John 13:34,35.

6. The installation of a "Jesus Chair" in a sanctuary can serve as a powerful reminder of Jesus' continuing presence, and of our call to reflect His manner of life and make Him visible. When people understand the significance of a "Jesus Chair," they should be encouraged to place one in their home, work place, classroom, etc.

7. A "Jesus Chair" can convey a powerful moral message. For example, suggest to young people that they can do whatever they like on a date, as long as they place a "Jesus Chair" nearby, or think of Jesus as sitting in the front seat of their car; they then commit themselves to do nothing that would cause Jesus sorrow and pain.

8. The question is always, "Are we causing Jesus to smile, or to weep?"

Also from Crossways International

❧ ***The Bible's Big Story—Our Story*** by Dr. Harry Wendt puts together the bits and pieces of the Bible's jigsaw. Using Crossways International's full-color time line and accompanying manual, you'll come to understand the Bible's overarching narratives and themes—not just a story here and there. You'll learn about the history of ancient Israel, discover the concerns of Old Testament writers, and find out how Jesus turned a lot of traditional thinking upside down. You'll be guided to Bible references that will introduce you to extraordinary places, people and events that might be new to you.

Your familiarity with the "big story" will also lead you to rediscover your own story. You'll find an answer to the question, "What does this long, complicated, sacred book mean to me, my family, my community?" The full-color time line that comes with this volume is also available as a wall chart and transparency. *The Bible's Big Story* can be purchased as a guided study on video cassette (VHS, 37 minutes). This course is ideal for individual, family or group study.

❧ ***See Through the Scriptures Video Series*** is another visual journey through the Bible's narrative, with a lot of new "scenery": 75 vivid and memorable illustrations. Dr. Harry Wendt uses these to guide you through the Old and New Testaments in sixteen 30-minute video sessions. Each session features an introduction by a moderator, a presentation of a topic by Dr. Wendt, and a wrap-up and question segment. You will be supplied with a colorful 84-page student manual to go along with the video. This series is an excellent basis for personal, family or group study.

To receive more information about Crossways International and our materials and seminars, please call the number at the bottom of the page. Or, fill out the form below, and send it to the address or fax number listed. We would be happy to send you our free catalogue, featuring Bible study courses, study Bibles, children's Bibles, Christian reference books and other products.

Name _____

Mailing Address _____

City _____ State _____ Zip _____

Telephone (   ) _____ (optional)

Mail this form to: *Or call or fax:*

Crossways International
7930 Computer Ave. So.   (612) 832-5454 (phone)
Minneapolis, MN 55435-5415   (612) 832-5553 (fax)
U.S.A.

IHN

PLEASE CONSIDER SHARING WHAT YOU HAVE LEARNED . . .

We read the paper, watch the television news, drive through poor neighborhoods. In the midst of a world that can make us feel sad and helpless, consider this confession of a former Puerto Rican drug king. He ended up in an Alaskan prison, where he attended a seminar designed by Crossways International:

> *Before coming to prison I have dreamed the same dream several times. I saw myself driving up in front of my sister's house in a shiny new car. When I stepped out I was dressed in a fine suit. Everyone was happy to see me because I had become a great success. Now I know that the dream will become a reality, but it will be through Christ that I will clothe myself and become a success in life. It will require His strength . . . all I have to do is "follow Him."*

Every year Crossways International leads thousands of people into the Bible where they discover their God-given mission: to restore people to unity with God and each other through Christ. We are active in more than forty countries—from Liberia, Estonia, Indonesia and Guatemala to churches, schools, prisons and special ministries in North America, Australia and New Zealand.

Wherever we go, we train local pastors and leaders to use our visual and written materials to teach the Bible to members of their community—from the illiterate to the educated. Crossways International's courses are used by more than thirty denominations around the world.

We can do this only because people like you have helped. If you would like someone else somewhere in the world to know and celebrate the wondrous message of the Bible, please consider a donation to Crossways International.

If you are able to send a gift of $30 or more, we would be pleased to send you a special Crossways International leather bookmark as a thank you for your partnership. Please check the appropriate box below.

Yes, I want to be part of the dynamic work of Crossways International to teach the Word of God so people can know Christ and live as His servants. Enclosed is a gift to help meet the needs of this crucial mission.

❑ $150   ❑ $100   ❑ $60   ❑ $30   ❑ other _____

❑ My gift is $30 or more; please send me the special Crossways International leather bookmark.

Please print the following information (if not included on your check).

Name _____

Street _____

City _____ State _____ Zip_____

Telephone (_____) _____ (optional)

Please cut off this portion of the page and mail it with your check (payable to *Crossways International*) to:
Crossways International
7930 Computer Ave. So.
Minneapolis, MN 55435-5415
U.S.A.

We are grateful for your prayers, encouragement and generous support.   IHN

Crossways International is a nonprofit organization. Contributions from U.S. donors are tax deductible.